ROYAL COURT

The Royal Court Theatre presents

DING DONG THE WICKED

by **Caryl Churchill**

DING DONG THE WICKED was first performed at The Royal Court Jerwood Theatre Downstairs, Sloane Square, on Monday 1st October 2012.

DING DONG THE WICKED

by Caryl Churchill

Cast in order of appearance
A Quiet Man/A Man Who Bites His Nails **John Marquez**
A Woman in Blue/A Drunk Woman **Sophie Stanton**
Young Woman Holding a Flower/
Young Woman with a Cigarette **Claire Foy**
An Overweight Man/A Man Who Is a Wreck **Stuart McQuarrie**
A Woman Who Bites/A Woman with a Limp **Jennie Stoller**
A Pale Young Man/A Speedy Young Man **Daniel Kendrick**

Director **Dominic Cooke**
Lighting Designer **Jack Williams**
Sound Designer **Alexander Caplen**
Casting Director **Amy Ball**
Assistant Director **Nick Bruckman**
Production Manager **Paul Handley**
Stage Manager **Richard Llewelyn**
Deputy Stage Manager **Hazel McDougall**
Costume Supervisor **Iona Kenrick**
Set built by **Footprint Scenery**

The Royal Court and Stage Management wish to thank Miriam Beuther & AV Repairs for their help with this production.

THE COMPANY

CARYL CHURCHILL (Writer)

FOR THE ROYAL COURT: Love & Information, Seven Jewish Children, Drunk Enough To Say I Love You?, A Number, Far Away, This is a Chair, Blue Heart, Mad Forest, Ice Cream, Serious Money, Fen, Top Girls, Cloud Nine, Traps, Light Shining In Buckinghamshire, Owners.

OTHER THEATRE INCLUDES: The Skriker (National).

MUSIC THEATRE INCLUDES: Lives of the Great Poisoners, Hotel (both with Orlando Gough).

Caryl has also written for radio & television.

NICK BRUCKMAN (Assistant Director)

AS DIRECTOR, THEATRE INCLUDES: Sister Of (Arcola); The Jonestown Project (Stratford East); It Gets Better (Oval House); Communication Breakdown (503); Miss Julie (Arcola, own translation); Hot Air (Edinburgh Festival Fringe); Friday (Drum, rehearsed reading, own translation).

AS ASSISTANT DIRECTOR, OTHER THEATRE INCLUDES: The Golden Dragon (ATC/Drum); Ich Werde Hier Sein im Sonnenschein und im Schatten (Staatstheater Stuttgart/Maxim Gorki, Berlin); Het Verhaal van Rain Man (De Utrechtse Spelen); Take Away (Stratford East).

Nick was a member of the 2011 Lincoln Center Directors Lab.

ALEXANDER CAPLEN (Sound Designer)

FOR THE ROYAL COURT: Goodbye to All That, Wanderlust, Over There (& Schaubühne, Berlin).

AS SOUND DESIGNER, OTHER THEATRE INCLUDES: Crave, Illusions, The Golden Dragon (ATC); Ogres (Tristan Bates); It's About Time (Nabokov); Mine, Ten Tiny Toes, War & Peace (Shared Experience); Stephen & the Sexy Partridge (Old Red Lion/ Trafalgar Studios), Peter Pan, Holes, Duck Variations (UK tour); The Wizard of Oz, The Entertainer (Nuffield); Imogen (Oval House/tour).

AS SOUND DESIGNER, OPERA INCLUDES: The Love for Three Oranges, Tosca (Grange Park Opera).

AS SOUND OPERATOR/ENGINEER, FOR THE ROYAL COURT: Wig Out!, Rhinoceros, The Arsonists, Free Outgoing, Now or Later, Gone Too Far, The Pain & the Itch.

AS SOUND OPERATOR/ENGINEER, OTHER THEATRE INCLUDES: Edinburgh Military Tattoo 2009 - present; Brontë, Kindertransport (Shared Experience); Blood Brothers (International tour); Ballroom (UK tour). Other work includes large-scale music touring as a Front of House mix engineer. Alex is Sound Deputy at the Royal Court & an Associate Artist (Sound) for ATC.

DOMINIC COOKE (Director)

FOR THE ROYAL COURT: Choir Boy, In Basildon, Chicken Soup with Barley, Clybourne Park (& Wyndham's); Aunt Dan & Lemon, The Fever, Seven Jewish Children, Wig Out!, Now or Later, War & Peace/Fear & Misery, Rhinoceros, The Pain & the Itch, Other People, Fireface, Spinning into Butter, Redundant, Fucking Games, Plasticine, The People Are Friendly, This is a Chair, Identical Twins.

OTHER THEATRE INCLUDES: Comedy of Errors (National); Arabian Nights, Pericles, The Winter's Tale, The Crucible, Postcards from America, As You Like It, Macbeth, Cymbeline, The Malcontent (RSC); By the Bog of Cats...(Wyndham's); The Eccentricities of a Nightingale (Gate, Dublin); Arabian Nights (Young Vic/UK & World Tours/New Victory Theatre, New York); The Weavers, Hunting Scenes from Lower Bavaria (Gate); The Bullet (Donmar); Afore Night Come, Entertaining Mr Sloane (Clwyd); The Importance of Being Earnest (Atlantic Theatre Festival, Canada); Caravan (National Theatre of Norway); My Mother Said I Never Should (Oxford Stage Co./Young Vic); Kiss of the Spider Woman (Bolton Octagon); Of Mice & Men (Nottingham Playhouse); Autogeddon (Assembly Rooms).

OPERA INCLUDES: The Magic Flute (WNO); I Capuleti e i Montecchi, La Bohème (Grange Park Opera).

AWARDS INCLUDE: Laurence Olivier Awards for Best Director & Best Revival for The Crucible; TMA Award for Arabian Nights; Fringe First Award for Autogeddon.

Dominic was Associate Director of the Royal Court 1999-2002, Associate Director of RSC 2002-2006 & Assistant Director RSC 1992-1993.

Dominic is Artistic Director of the Royal Court.

CLAIRE FOY (Young Woman Holding a Flower/Young Woman with a Cigarette)

FOR THE ROYAL COURT: Love, Love, Love.

OTHER THEATRE INCLUDES: DNA/The Miracle/Baby Girl (National).

TELEVISION INCLUDES: Upstairs Downstairs, Hacks, White Heat, The Night Watch, The Promise, Going Postal, Pulse, Little Dorrit, Being Human.

FILM INCLUDES: Wreckers, Season of the Witch.

DANIEL KENDRICK (A Pale Young Man/A Speedy Young Man)

FOR THE ROYAL COURT: Vera Vera Vera.

OTHER THEATRE INCLUDES: Rosie & Jim (Mobculture); Chapel Street (Liverpool Playhouse/Old Red Lion); Coalition (503).

TELEVISION INCLUDES: EastEnders, 999, Run.

FILM INCLUDES: Offender, Lovebite.

STUART MCQUARRIE (An Overweight Man/A Man Who Is a Wreck)

FOR THE ROYAL COURT: Wanderlust, Relocated, Cleansed, Clybourne Park (Wyndham's).

THEATRE INCLUDES: Detroit, King James Bible Readings, Happy Now?, Scenes from the Big Picture, Ivanov (National); Marble (Abbey); Realism (National Theatre of Scotland/EIF); The God of Hell, The Dark, The Life of Stuff (Donmar); The Taming of the Shrew (RSC); Our Country's Good (Out of Joint/International tour); Shining Souls (Old Vic); The Government Inspector (Almeida); The Slab Boys Trilogy (Young Vic); Macbeth (Tron/Dundee Rep); The Thrie Estaites (EIF); Shining Souls, The House Among the Stars, The Life of Stuff, Hardie & Baird, Ines De Castro, Clocked Out, Loose Ends (Traverse); City Lights (PDB); A Midsummer Night's Dream (TAG); Laurel & Hardy, Good Morning Bill, Arsenic & Old Lace, The Bevellers, The Comedians, The Country Wife, Look Back in Anger, The Slab Boys, Mother Courage, Death of a Salesman, Charlie's Aunt, The Merchant of Venice, The Glass Menagerie, Hay Fever (Royal Lyceum); The Snow Queen (Dundee Rep).

TELEVISION INCLUDES: The Fuse, Hustle, Lip Service, Any Human Heart, The Bill, Silent Witness, Extras Christmas Special, Whistleblowers, Peep Show, Taggart, Rebus, Black Book, A Very Social Secretary, Ghost Squad, Marian, Again, Golden Hour, Box of Slice, Life Begins, The Deal, The Way We Live Now, Four Fathers, The Echo, Butterfly Collectors, Silent Witness, Invasion Earth, London's Burning, The Peter Principle, Doctor Finlay, Taggart, Casualty, Hamish Macbeth, The High Life, Strathblair, City Lights, Ines de Castro, Loose Ends, The Justice Game, The Continental.

FILM INCLUDES: Blood, Closer to the Moon, Isle of Dogs, Burke & Hare, Another Year, House in Berlin, Franklyn, Hush, Young Adam, 28 Days Later, The Honeytrap, The Life of Stuff, Trainspotting, Love Me Tender.

JOHN MARQUEZ (A Quiet Man/A Man Who Bites His Nails)

FOR THE ROYAL COURT: Mother Teresa is Dead, Identical Twins, Local.

THEATRE INCLUDES: Ragtime (Regent's Park); The Taming of the Shrew (RSC); House of Games, Chain Play II, The Hypochondriac (Almeida); A Flea in Her Ear (Old Vic); Annie Get Your Gun (Young Vic); The Dark Side of Buffoon (Lyric Hammersmith); The Good Soul of Szechuan (Young Vic); House of Games, The Emperor Jones, Market Boy, Sing Yer Heart Out for the Lads (National); The Anniversary (Garrick).

TELEVISION INCLUDES: Doc Martin, Hotel Babylon, Suburban Shootout, Ronni Ancona & Co.

SOPHIE STANTON (A Woman in Blue/A Drunk Woman)

THEATRE INCLUDES: The Knot of the Heart, Cloud Nine, Dying For It (Almedia); England People Very Nice, Market Boy (National); Mercury Fur, Sleeping Around (Paines Plough); Breeze Block Park (Liverpool Playhouse); Bright (Soho); Top Girls (BAC); Crossing The Equator, Beautiful Thing (& Donmar), Backstroke in a Crowded Pool (Bush); A Collier's Friday Night (Hampstead); Hindle Wakes, Love's Labour's Lost (Royal Exchange, Manchester); Slaughter City (RSC).

TELEVISION INCLUDES: May Day, The Silent & the Damned, EastEnders, One Night, Midsomer Murders, Lewis, Outnumbered, Ashes to Ashes, Hunter, Wallander, Whitechapel, Silent Witness, Sold, Jekyll, Spitgame, Our Hidden Lives, Fingersmith, Wall of Silence, The Brief, Coupling, The Vice, Hidden City, Girl's Night, Tough Love, Black Books, The Mayor of Casterbridge, Prime Suspect, Gimme Gimme Gimme, A Touch of Frost, Plastic Man, The Wilsons, Dressing For Breakfast, Where The Heart Is, The Unknown Soldier, The Sculptress, Plain Jane, Dangerous Lady, Shine on Harvey Moon, Peak Practice.

FILM INCLUDES: How I Live Now, Cheerful Weather for the Wedding, Grow Your Own, Linger, Beautiful Thing, Shadowlands.

JENNIE STOLLER (A Woman Who Bites/A Woman with a Limp)

FOR THE ROYAL COURT: Seven Jewish Children, Cries from the Mammal House, Fen (& Almeida/Public, NYC), Action.

THEATRE INCLUDES: Hacked (503); Scorched (Old Vic Tunnels); Three Sisters on Hope Street (Liverpool Everyman/Hampstead); Woyzeck (Gate); The Oedipus Plays, The Mountain Giants, Harliquinade, The Elephant Man (National); Ion (National Studio); The Castle (Riverside/International tour); The Europeans (Greenwich/UK tour); At Fifty She Discovered the Sea (Liverpool Playhouse Studio); Brighton Beach Memoirs (West Yorkshire Playhouse); The House of Bernada Alba (Royal Lyceum); The Beaux Stratagem, A Midsummer Night's Dream (RSC/tour); The Henrys (ESC Old Vic/tour); Heartbreak House (Shared Experience); Sons of Light (Newcastle Playhouse); The Speakers (Joint Stock); Peter Brook's A Midsummer Night's Dream (RSC world tour).

TELEVISION INCLUDES: Casualty 1909, Casualty, In Defence, McLibel, Bliss, The Way We Used to Live, Scot & the Arms Antics, One Foot in the Grave, The Bill, Love Hurts, Shrinks, Sapphire & Steel, Eleanor Marx.

FILM INCLUDES: Genghis Khan, The Good Father, King Ralph.

RADIO INCLUDES: Jago & Litefoot, The Wandering Jew, Seven Wonders of the Divided World, The Adulteries of a Provincial Wife, Amongst the Medici, Shylock, Writer Christmas: Grotto, From Paradise to Heaven, Miss Morrison's Ghosts, The Schartz-Metterklume Method, Love III, Every Eye, Maigret & the Burglar's Wife, Element of Water, Love II, Stalingrad, The Slap, His Dark Materials: The Amber Spyglass, Bunn & Co, Passover, The Aerodrome.

Jennie was a member of the BBC Radio Drama Company.

AWARDS INCLUDE: Best Actress in a Visiting Production for The Castle, Manchester Evening News.

JACK WILLIAMS (Lighting Designer)

AS RE-LIGHTER, FOR THE ROYAL COURT: Vera Vera Vera.

AS LIGHTING DESIGNER, THEATRE INCLUDES: Cowardy Custard, Les Misérables (Canterbury Marlowe); The Storm, The Killing Game (BAC); Book Of Little Things (Oval House).

AS ASSOCIATE LIGHTING DESIGNER, THEATRE INCLUDES: Ragtime, A Midsummer's Night Dream (Regent's Park).

AS PRODUCTION LX/RE-LIGHTER, OTHER THEATRE INCLUDES: Scrooge: The Musical, Half a Sixpence (UK tours); Joseph & the Amazing Technicolor Dreamcoat (Japan); Opera Holland Park; La Cage Aux Folles (Playhouse); Dreamboats & Petticoats (Savoy/Playhouse/UK tour); Swallows & Amazons (Vaudeville); Plague Over England (The Duchess); Pleasance 2007-2011 (Edinburgh).

AS ASSISTANT LIGHTING DESIGNER, OPERA INCLUDES: The Magic Flute, Albert Herring (British Youth Opera).

AS PRODUCTION LX, OPERA INCLUDES: Don Pasquale, L'Amico Fritz (Opera Holland Park).

Jack is Head of Lighting at the Royal Court Theatre.

THE ENGLISH STAGE COMPANY
AT THE ROYAL COURT THEATRE

'For me the theatre is really a religion or way of life. You must decide what you feel the world is about and what you want to say about it, so that everything in the theatre you work in is saying the same thing ... A theatre must have a recognisable attitude. It will have one, whether you like it or not.'

George Devine, first artistic director of the English Stage Company: notes for an unwritten book.

photo: Stephen Cummiskey

As Britain's leading national company dedicated to new work, the Royal Court Theatre produces new plays of the highest quality, working with writers from all backgrounds, and addressing the problems and possibilities of our time.

"The Royal Court has been at the centre of British cultural life for the past 50 years, an engine room for new writing and constantly transforming the theatrical culture." Stephen Daldry

Since its foundation in 1956, the Royal Court has presented premieres by almost every leading contemporary British playwright, from John Osborne's Look Back in Anger to Caryl Churchill's A Number and Tom Stoppard's Rock 'n' Roll. Just some of the other writers to have chosen the Royal Court to premiere their work include Edward Albee, John Arden, Richard Bean, Samuel Beckett, Edward Bond, Leo Butler, Jez Butterworth, Martin Crimp, Ariel Dorfman, Stella Feehily, Christopher Hampton, David Hare, Eugène Ionesco, Ann Jellicoe, Terry Johnson, Sarah Kane, David Mamet, Martin McDonagh, Conor McPherson, Joe Penhall, Lucy Prebble, Mark Ravenhill, Simon Stephens, Wole Soyinka, Polly Stenham, David Storey, Debbie Tucker Green, Arnold Wesker and Roy Williams.

"It is risky to miss a production there." Financial Times

In addition to its full-scale productions, the Royal Court also facilitates international work at a grass roots level, developing exchanges which bring young writers to Britain and sending British writers, actors and directors to work with artists around the world. The research and play development arm of the Royal Court Theatre, The Studio, finds the most exciting and diverse range of new voices in the UK. The Studio runs play-writing groups including the Young Writers Programme, Critical Mass for black, Asian and minority ethnic writers and the biennial Young Writers Festival. For further information, go to www.royalcourttheatre.com/playwriting/the-studio.

"Yes, the Royal Court is on a roll. Yes, Dominic Cooke has just the genius and kick that this venue needs... It's fist-bitingly exciting." Independent

Jerwood Theatre Downstairs

Until 13 Oct

love and information by Caryl Churchill

In this fast moving kaleidoscope more than a hundred characters try to make sense of what they know.

25 Oct – 24 Nov

NSFW by Lucy Kirkwood

A sharp new comedy looking at power games and privacy in the media and beyond.

6 Dec – 19 Jan

in the republic of happiness by Martin Crimp

A provocative roll-call of contemporary obsessions.

Jerwood Theatre Upstairs

18 Oct – 17 Nov

the river by Jez Butterworth

The writer and director behind *Jerusalem* return with a bewitching new story.

12 – 17 Nov

new plays from india
International Playwrights: A Genesis Foundation Project

A week of readings from five original and contemporary voices

23 Nov – 22 Dec

hero by E. V. Crowe

A bracing new story of a heroic modern man.
Hero is part of the Royal Court's Jerwood New Playwrights programme, supported by the Jerwood Charitable Foundation.

Royal Court Theatre Productions and Ambassador Theatre Group present

Royal Court at the Duke of York's. St Martin's Lane, WC2N 4BG

Until 3 Nov

jumpy
by April De Angelis

Tamsin Greig reprises her critically acclaimed role.

9 Nov – 5 Jan

constellations
by Nick Payne

Sally Hawkins and Rafe Spall perform in this explosive new play.

020 7565 5000
www.royalcourttheatre.com

⊖ Sloane Square ⇄ Victoria ☐ royalcourt ☐ theroyalcourttheatre

Principal Sponsor **Coutts**

Supported by
ARTS COUNCIL
ENGLAND

ROYAL COURT SUPPORTERS

The Royal Court has significant and longstanding relationships with many organisations and individuals who provide vital support. It is this support that makes possible its unique playwriting and audience development programmes.

Coutts is the Principal Sponsor of the Royal Court. The Genesis Foundation supports the Royal Court's work with International Playwrights. Theatre Local is sponsored by Bloomberg. The Jerwood Charitable Foundation supports new plays by playwrights through the Jerwood New Playwrights series. The Andrew Lloyd Webber Foundation supports the Royal Court's Studio, which aims to seek out, nurture and support emerging playwrights. Over the past ten years the BBC has supported the Gerald Chapman Fund for directors.

The Harold Pinter Playwright's Award is given annually by his widow, Lady Antonia Fraser, to support a new commission at the Royal Court.

PUBLIC FUNDING
Arts Council England, London
British Council
European Commission Representation in the UK

CHARITABLE DONATIONS
Martin Bowley Charitable Trust
Gerald Chapman Fund
Columbia Foundation
Cowley Charitable Trust
The Dorset Foundation
The John Ellerman Foundation
The Eranda Foundation
Genesis Foundation
J Paul Getty Jnr Charitable Trust
The Golden Bottle Trust
The Haberdashers' Company
Paul Hamlyn Foundation
Jerwood Charitable Foundation
Marina Kleinwort Charitable Trust
The Andrew Lloyd Webber Foundation
John Lyon's Charity
The Andrew W Mellon Foundation
The David & Elaine Potter Foundation
Rose Foundation
Royal Victoria Hall Foundation
The Dr Mortimer & Theresa Sackler Foundation
John Thaw Foundation
The Vandervell Foundation
The Garfield Weston Foundation

CORPORATE SUPPORTERS & SPONSORS
BBC
Bloomberg
Coutts
Ecosse Films
Kudos Film & Television
MAC
Moët & Chandon
Oakley Capital Limited
Smythson of Bond Street
White Light Ltd

BUSINESS ASSOCIATES, MEMBERS & BENEFACTORS
Auerbach & Steele Opticians
Bank of America Merrill Lynch
Hugo Boss
Lazard
Peter Jones
Savills
Vanity Fair

DEVELOPMENT ADVOCATES
John Ayton MBE
Elizabeth Bandeen
Kinvara Balfour
Anthony Burton CBE
Piers Butler
Sindy Caplan
Sarah Chappatte
Cas Donald (Vice Chair)
Celeste Fenichel
Emma Marsh (Chair)
Deborah Shaw Marquardt (Vice Chair)
Sian Westerman
Nick Wheeler
Daniel Winterfeldt

Supported by
ARTS COUNCIL ENGLAND

INDIVIDUAL MEMBERS

GROUND-BREAKERS

Anonymous
Moira Andreae
Allen Appen & Jane West
Mr & Mrs Simon Andrews
Nick Archdale
Charlotte Asprey
Jane Attias
Brian Balfour-Oatts
Elizabeth & Adam Bandeen
Ray Barrell
Dr Kate Best
Stan & Val Bond
Kristina Borsy & Nick Turdean
Neil & Sarah Brener
Mrs Deborah Brett
Mrs Joanna Buckhenham
Clive & Helena Butler
Sindy & Jonathan Caplan
Gavin & Lesley Casey
Sarah & Philippe Chappatte
Tim & Caroline Clark
Christine Collins
Carole & Neville Conrad
Anthony & Andrea Coombs
Clyde Cooper
Ian & Caroline Cormack
Mr & Mrs Cross
Andrew & Amanda Cryer
Alison Davies
Matthew Dean
Roger & Alison De Haan
Noel De Keyzer
Polly Devlin OBE
Glen Donovan
Denise & Randolph Dumas
Robyn Durie
Zeina Durra & Saadi Soudavar
Glenn & Phyllida Earle
The Edwin Fox Foundation
Mark & Sarah Evans
Margaret Exley CBE
Leonie Fallstrom
Celeste & Peter Fenichel
John Garfield
Beverley Gee
Mr & Mrs Georgiades
Nick & Julie Gould
Lord & Lady Grabiner
Richard & Marcia Grand
Don & Sue Guiney
Jill Hackel & Andrzej Zarzycki
Carol Hall
Jennifer & Stephen Harper
Sam & Caroline Haubold
Anoushka Healy
Madeleine Hodgkin
Mr & Mrs Gordon Holmes
Damien Hyland
The David Hyman Charitable Trust
Amanda Ibbetson
Nicholas Jones
David Kaskel & Christopher Teano
Vincent & Amanda Keaveny
Peter & Maria Kellner
Nicola Kerr
Philip & Joan Kingsley
Mr & Mrs Pawel Kisielewski
Sarah & David Kowitz
Rosemary Leith
Larry & Peggy Levy
Imelda Liddiard
Daisy & Richard Littler
Kathryn Ludlow
Dr Ekaterina Malievskaia & George Goldsmith
Christopher Marek Rencki
Andy McIver
Barbara Minto
Shafin & Angelie Moledina
Ann & Gavin Neath CBE
Murray North
Clive & Annie Norton
Georgia Oetker
Mr & Mrs Guy Patterson
William Plapinger & Cassie Murray
Andrea & Hilary Ponti
Lauren Prakke
Annie & Preben Prebensen
Julie Ritter
Mark & Tricia Robinson
Paul & Gill Robinson
Sir & Lady Ruddock
William & Hilary Russell
Julie & Bill Ryan
Sally & Anthony Salz
Bhags Sharma
The Michael & Melanie Sherwood Charitable Foundation
Tom Siebens & Mimi Parsons
Andy Simpkin
Anthony Simpson & Susan Boster
Paul & Rita Skinner
Mr & Mrs RAH Smart
Brian Smith
Mr Michael Spencer
Sue St Johns
The Ulrich Family
The Ury Trust
Amanda Vail
Constance Von Unruh
Ian & Victoria Watson
Matthew & Sian Westerman

BOUNDARY-BREAKERS

Katie Bradford
Piers & Melanie Gibson
David Harding
Steve Kingshott
Emma Marsh
Philippa Thorp
Mr & Mrs Nick Wheeler

MOVER-SHAKERS

Eric Abraham
Anonymous
Mr & Mrs Ayton MBE
Lloyd & Sarah Dorfman
Lydia & Manfred Gorvy
Mr & Mrs Roderick Jack
Duncan Matthews QC
Miles Morland
Ian & Carol Sellars
Edgar & Judith Wallner

MAJOR DONORS

Rob & Siri Cope
Cas Donald
Jack & Linda Keenan
Deborah & Stephen Marquardt
NoraLee & Jon Sedmak
Jan & Michael Topham
Stuart & Hilary Williams Charitable Foundation

Thank you to all our Friends, Stage-Takers and Ice-Breakers for their generous support.

DING DONG THE WICKED

Caryl Churchill

Characters
in order of appearance

1.

A QUIET MAN, *forty-five*
A WOMAN IN BLUE, *late forties*
A YOUNG WOMAN CARRYING A FLOWER,
    twenties, girlfriend of the pale young man
AN OVERWEIGHT MAN, *fifty-plus, husband of the woman
    in blue, brother of the quiet man*
A WOMAN WHO BITES, *seventies, mother of the overweight
    man and the quiet man*
A PALE YOUNG MAN, *twenties, a soldier, son of the
    overweight man and the woman in blue*

2.

A YOUNG WOMAN WITH A CIGARETTE, *twenties*
A MAN WHO BITES HIS NAILS, *forty-five, her husband*
A DRUNK WOMAN, *late forties, her mother*
A WOMAN WITH A LIMP, *seventies, her grandmother*
A SPEEDY YOUNG MAN, *twenties, a soldier, brother of the
    man who bites his nails*
A MAN WHO IS A WRECK, *fifty-plus, a neighbour*

The actors double the parts.

Place

1. A living room.

2. A living room in another country.

This text went to press before the end of rehearsals and so may differ slightly from the play as performed.

1.

A living room. There is a door leading to the rest of the house, a front door and a window. There is a tv but we can't see the screen or hear the sound.

A QUIET MAN, *about forty-five, is alone in the room. There is a plastic sheet on the floor and a large strong bin bag.*

Doorbell. The QUIET MAN *opens the front door, taking out a gun.*

QUIET MAN   Come in.

                    The QUIET MAN *shoots someone, who falls dead. The* QUIET MAN *puts the body and the bloodstained plastic sheet in the bag, and leaves with the bag by the front door.*

                    Time passes.

                    Doorbell. A WOMAN IN BLUE, *late forties, comes from inside and opens the street door. A* YOUNG WOMAN CARRYING A FLOWER *comes in, they embrace.*

YW *w* FLOWER   All right?

W *in* BLUE   I am, he is, guess who's making a fuss. Just don't get him started.

FLOWER   It's because he's suffered, isn't it, I know he has.

BLUE   I get tired of it.

FLOWER   Of course.

BLUE   I'm not saying he's wrong.

FLOWER   You're sensible, that's what it is.

BLUE   Mind you.

FLOWER   Oh I'm not saying…

BLUE   There's someone kept calling me
                names when I was at school,
                jellybelly, doubletrouble – just a bit
                overweight – and one day I pushed
                her so she fell down in a puddle and
                before she could get herself sorted
                out I jumped right on her and I got
                a handful of mud and stuffed it in
                her mouth.

FLOWER   She was asking for it.

BLUE   She was pretty but she was skinny.
                She's the one with the problem.

FLOWER   Did I hear someone crying?

BLUE   She's just calming down. You can't
                let them think they've got you
                where they want you. You have to
                break their spirit. It doesn't take
                long.

                An OVERWEIGHT MAN, *about
                fifty, husband of the woman in blue, enters
                from indoors and goes to the window.*

OVERWEIGHT   What's happened?

BLUE   We keep watch all the time so they
                don't get away with anything.

FLOWER   Is it bad?

BLUE   Music day and night.

FLOWER   They're such beautiful trees too.

OVERWEIGHT   Bastards. Bastards. They want to destroy us.

BLUE   (*To* FLOWER.) I did tell you.

OVERWEIGHT   I'll kill them. Help me.

BLUE   Everything's all right. It's all right. We have a visitor.

OVERWEIGHT   Come to see him off, have you? He's going to be a hero. It's a big cause. Is he a big enough man?

BLUE   (*To* FLOWER.) He's in his room. He'd like to see you.

                The YOUNG WOMAN CARRYING A FLOWER *exits indoors.*

                She's not crying any more. Shall I get her?

OVERWEIGHT   I've something to say to you.

BLUE   You've nothing to say, I know what you get up to.

OVERWEIGHT   It's not surprising, I'm not the one who started this.

BLUE   I'm not the one breaking up our marriage, don't try and put it on me.

OVERWEIGHT	You want to break it up, do you?
BLUE	I didn't say that.
OVERWEIGHT	You want it, you can have it, it's your idea remember that.
BLUE	No one could blame me. I've been hurt. You're a monster. Just let it go. I'm past caring now.
OVERWEIGHT	What's happening out there?
BLUE	Another thing, I've had enough of your brother. He's a criminal. I don't need this. And drinking again.
OVERWEIGHT	He's not staying forever.
BLUE	How long's forever? How long's he not staying for?
OVERWEIGHT	Will you stop shouting at me?
BLUE	I didn't raise my voice. Did I raise my voice?
OVERWEIGHT	I'm not listening.
BLUE	I know you're not.
OVERWEIGHT	It's his last day. It could be a peaceful time.
BLUE	And whose fault is it? I'm basically a very peaceful person.
OVERWEIGHT	You?
BLUE	Aren't I?
OVERWEIGHT	Yes, you are.

BLUE	I'm what?
OVERWEIGHT	A peaceful person. Am I? What do you think?
BLUE	Yes.
OVERWEIGHT	Good. You have to forgive me because I mean well.
BLUE	There then. There, my dear. Shall we let her out?
OVERWEIGHT	No, let's have some peace.

The QUIET MAN *lets himself in through the front door. He is the brother of the overweight man.*

QUIET MAN	Gone?
BLUE	He'll be down in a minute.
QUIET MAN	Drink?
BLUE	You drink too much.
QUIET MAN	Drink?
BLUE	Might as well.
QUIET MAN	Bastard came up on the inside so I cut in front to show him and he nearly drove me off the road.
BLUE	(*To* OVERWEIGHT.) Go and get him. I want to see him.
OVERWEIGHT	I was about fifteen, there was a dead dog, the body was by the road, and I thought, asleep, no, that's dead, it was getting squashy, there

was a lot of flies, and I thought that's really dead, and I suddenly thought I could do that, if it really helped my country and what I believe in and the people I love and our way of life which is threatened, if I could take some of those bastards with me I could be really happy to be dead, except I didn't expect to be happy, I expect to be nothing, but happy to do something that could make me end up dead, I could do that.

The OVERWEIGHT MAN *goes by the inside door.*

QUIET MAN   You know what he did.

BLUE   I don't want to talk about that.

QUIET MAN   Nobody talks about that.

BLUE   He always tells that story.

QUIET MAN   Yes, that's the bit he tells.

Pause.

BLUE   We mustn't.

QUIET MAN   I know but we have to.

BLUE   He's just as bad.

QUIET MAN   He's insane.

BLUE   Oh god, I want you so much.

QUIET MAN   I want you so much.

BLUE   I want you so much too.

A WOMAN WHO BITES, *seventies, mother of the overweight man and the quiet man, enters from indoors.*

W WHO BITES	Where is he?
BLUE	He'll be down in a minute.
QUIET MAN	Drink?
BITES	Are we celebrating? Celebrating sending another one off to be killed?
BLUE	Celebrating maybe he'll kill some of them.
BITES	My darling was completely destroyed. There was nothing left.
BLUE	Yes, don't get excited.
BITES	They've got graves to go to, you stupid child. Killing's not enough.

The OVERWEIGHT MAN *comes back in.*

OVERWEIGHT	There's nothing I inherited except my father's hair and his lefthandedness. Everything I got I earned. And the government want to take that away. The hero's coming.
BLUE	I'm going to let her out.
OVERWEIGHT	I said no.
QUIET MAN	Is she shut in her room again?
BLUE	Her parents know what to do, thank you.

A PALE YOUNG MAN, *son of the overweight man and the woman in blue, and the* YOUNG WOMAN CARRYING A FLOWER *enter from indoors. He is wearing military uniform and holding the flower.*

BITES	Here we are.
OVERWEIGHT	Have you ever seen a man dead?
QUIET MAN	(*Offering*) Drink?
PALE YM	It's fine because I believe in what we're doing.
BITES	You're a good boy.
OVERWEIGHT	His grandfather was a missionary. He gave his life bringing the truth.
FLOWER	I do think it's right to try to be good.
BLUE	You're drinking too much.
QUIET MAN	And?
OVERWEIGHT	That's the most important thing, a clear conscience.
BITES	They're pus you have to kill with disinfectant. Vermin.
QUIET MAN	Drink?
BLUE	(*To* FLOWER.) They want to build ugly little houses right in the middle of the view. It's lovely there. It's ancient. I won't take it. I'm not the type.

BITES   (*To* FLOWER.) Did you know my
               son was killed? Do you know about
               it?

FLOWER   Yes, I'm sorry.

OVERWEIGHT   So you're here to say goodbye.

FLOWER   Yes, I keep crying.

PALE   She'll forget all about me.

FLOWER   He doesn't mean that.

PALE   It's my beautiful country, that's what
               it is.

BLUE   Listen. Listen.

OVERWEIGHT   Listen. Look. Blood

               *They all turn to the tv. We can't see the
               screen or hear what's said. They listen and
               look, then explode in triumph.*

               Dead.

BLUE   Yes!

FLOWER   What?

QUIET MAN   They've got him.

BITES   He's dead.

BLUE   Did you hear that?

OVERWEIGHT   Like a dog.

PALE   Yaaay.

               *They all start a chant, which goes on for
               some time, continuing while other things
               are said.*

ALL	Zig zig zig, zag zag zag, zig zig zig, zag zag zag…
BITES	Oh god oh god oh god
BLUE	(*To* PALE.) Specially for you.
OVERWEIGHT	Go go go.

The chant dies down, laughter.

FLOWER	I can't help feeling
QUIET MAN	This calls for a drink. Shall we let her out?
OVERWEIGHT	Listen!

The OVERWEIGHT MAN *goes to the window.*

Look! The trees!

The OVERWEIGHT MAN *rushes off indoors (to the garden) followed by the* WOMAN IN BLUE *and the* QUIET MAN.

PALE	Can't help feeling what?
FLOWER	Nothing.
PALE	What?
FLOWER	A bit sorry for him.
PALE	I can. Do you love me?
FLOWER	Yes. Do you love me?
PALE	Yes. That's good then.
BITES	Where's everyone gone?

FLOWER   I think people should try to forgive
                each other.

PALE   We can't do that.

FLOWER   No, I know.

PALE   I'll tell you something. If you love
                me.

FLOWER   What?

BITES   What are you whispering about?

FLOWER   Tell me.

PALE   I don't want to do it. I don't think I
                can do it.

FLOWER   You can.

PALE   I don't want to.

                The QUIET MAN *comes back.*

QUIET MAN   False alarm. Want a drink?

PALE   Not now.

FLOWER   Yes, please.

QUIET   (*To* PALE.) You'll get drunk a lot if
                you get the chance.

BITES   There's my brave boy. Bite.

FLOWER   I'm sorry, I can't stop crying.

PALE   Zig zig zig.

2.

Another country. A living room. It is identical and the furniture is identical except it's in different positions.

A MAN WHO BITES HIS NAILS, *about forty-five, and a* YOUNG WOMAN WITH A CIGARETTE.

YW *w* CIG	It's a big cause.
MAN NAILS	Have you ever seen a man dead?
CIG	Will you stop shouting at me?
NAILS	Did I raise my voice?
CIG	I'm not the one breaking up our marriage.
NAILS	You want it to break up, do you?
CIG	I get tired of it.
NAILS	I do think it's right to try to be good.
CIG	Do you love me?
NAILS	Yes.
CIG	It's my beautiful country, that's what it is.
NAILS	Do you love me?
CIG	What do you think?
NAILS	I want you so much.
CIG	I want you so much too.

NAILS	He'll be down in a minute.
CIG	I've had enough of your brother.
NAILS	He's insane.
CIG	He's going to be a hero.
NAILS	You know what he did?

Doorbell. The YOUNG WOMAN WITH A CIGARETTE *opens the street door and a* DRUNK WOMAN, *late forties, her mother, and a* WOMAN WITH A LIMP, *seventies, her grandmother, come in, embracing her.*

DRUNK W	Here we are.
CIG	Come to see him off? He's in his room.
NAILS	Drink?
DRUNK	Are we celebrating? I am.
WOMAN *w* LIMP	Did I hear crying? Is she shut in her room again?
CIG	She's the one with a problem.
DRUNK	Bastard came up on the inside so I cut in front to show him and he nearly drove me off the road. There was a dead dog.
NAILS	You?
DRUNK	No one could blame me.
CIG	Drinking again.
DRUNK	I don't want to talk about that.

CIG	No, I know.
DRUNK	Guess who's making a fuss. You drink too much.
LIMP	She's not crying any more.
CIG	Her parents know what to do, thank you.
	A SPEEDY YOUNG MAN, *brother of the man who bites his nails, enters from indoors. He is wearing a military uniform, not the same as the pale young man wore in 1.*
DRUNK	The hero's coming.
SPEEDY YM	So you're here to say goodbye.
DRUNK	Celebrating. You're a good boy. Maybe he'll kill some of them.
NAILS	Don't get excited.
SPEEDY	I'll kill them all right.
CIG	Killing's not enough.
SPEEDY	Drink?
DRUNK	Let's. It's his last day.
CIG	We keep watch all the time so they can't get away with anything. You can't let them think they've got you where they want you. They're vermin.
NAILS	I can't help feeling…
CIG	What?

NAILS	Nothing. Just let it go.
CIG	I'm not the one that started this. Don't try and put it on me.
NAILS	I didn't say that.
CIG	I believe in what we're doing.
LIMP	Shall we let her out? Shall I get her?
CIG	There's someone kept calling me names when I was at school, I was about fifteen, and one day I jumped right on her.
SPEEDY	Bastards.
CIG	You have to break their spirit.
SPEEDY	The body was by the road right in the middle of the view and I thought, that's dead, that's really dead, it was getting squashy, there was a lot of flies, and I suddenly thought I could do that if it really helped my country, if I could take some of those bastards out.
CIG	I could do that.
NAILS	You want it.
SPEEDY	I'm basically a very peaceful person. But we have to.
CIG	I know.
DRUNK	There's my brave boy. He is.
SPEEDY	There was nothing left. She was asking for it. She fell down. And

	before she could get herself sorted out, I stuffed it in her mouth. I don't expect to be happy. But happy to do something.
NAILS	And that's the bit he tells. I know what you get up to. You're a monster.
CIG	He doesn't mean that.
SPEEDY	I'm what?
CIG	He's just as bad.
NAILS	Am I?
CIG	Yes, you are. Nobody talks about that.
SPEEDY	A clear conscience?
CIG	A peaceful person. (*To* NAILS.) You've nothing to say.
NAILS	If I did…
SPEEDY	Is it bad?
NAILS	Of course.
SPEEDY	It's not surprising. Tell me.
NAILS	I don't think I can.
CIG	Mind you, I'm not saying he's wrong. It's fine because…
NAILS	Because I mean well?
DRUNK	What are you whispering about? Do you know they want to build ugly little houses? They're such beautiful

trees too. And the government wants to take that away. Bastards. Everything I earned.

CIG   You're drinking too much. I'm not listening.

DRUNK   What do you know about it, you stupid child? There's nothing I inherited except my father's lefthandedness.

LIMP   And his hair.

DRUNK   Can't help feeling what… Our way of life. It's the trees. And what I believe in, which is threatened.

LIMP   Yes, that's the most important thing.

DRUNK   I keep crying.

LIMP   (*Of* DRUNK.) Everything's all right. She's just calming down.

DRUNK   Bastards. I'll tell you something. You have to kill.

CIG   Drink, drink, specially for you. You can have it. Get drunk. I'm past caring.

NAILS   Listen.

CIG   What's happened?

SPEEDY   Listen. Look. They've got him.

They all turn to the tv. We can't see the screen or hear what's said. They listen and look then explode in triumph.

DRUNK	Oh.
LIMP	Gone.
SPEEDY	Dead.
CIG	That's dead, that's really dead.
NAILS	Did you hear that?
DRUNK	Dog.
	They all start a chant which goes on for some time, continuing while other things are said.
ALL	Zig zig zig, zag zag zag, zig zig zig, zag zag zag…
DRUNK	Drink.
SPEEDY	(*To* CIG *secretly.*) I want you so much
CIG	(*To* SPEEDY *secretly.*) I said no.
LIMP	He's dead. Oh god.
SPEEDY	(*To* CIG *secretly.*) You're sensible, that's what it is.
DRUNK	Go go go.
	The chant dies down, laughter.
NAILS	This calls for a drink.
DRUNK	Celebrating.
NAILS	It could be a peaceful time now.
CIG	No, it's ancient.
NAILS	I think people should try to forgive each other.

SPEEDY   Is he a big enough man to forgive
                me?

LIMP   (*Aside to* DRUNK.) Shall we let her
                out? I'm going to let her out.

DRUNK   (*Aside to* LIMP.) You're not. We
                mustn't. We can't do that.

LIMP   (*Aside to* DRUNK.) I can.

NAILS   (*To* SPEEDY.) Might as well.

CIG   That's good then. And?

SPEEDY   I'm not the type.

                *Banging about outside then banging at the
                front door and ringing of doorbell. The*
                WOMAN WITH A LIMP *gets up
                unnoticed except by the* DRUNK
                WOMAN *and exits indoors.*

                What's happening out there?

                The SPEEDY YOUNG MAN
                produces a gun.

NAILS   No. It's your idea.

                More banging at the door.

DRUNK   Oh god.

                The MAN WHO BITES HIS
                NAILS *opens the front door. A* MAN
                WHO IS A WRECK *comes in. He is
                very bedraggled and carries various bags
                full of possessions. The* SPEEDY
                YOUNG MAN *puts the gun away.*

CIG   False alarm. We have a visitor.

NAILS	It's all right. I did tell you.
WRECK	(*Of himself.*) He'd like to see you.
SPEEDY	Just don't get him started.
CIG	He's not staying. Not now.
WRECK	Aren't I? I've something to say to you.
DRUNK	It's because he's suffered isn't it.
CIG	I know he has. He's a criminal.
DRUNK	A bit sorry for him. His grandfather was a missionary.
WRECK	Listen. My darling was completely destroyed. It doesn't take long. A puddle. Blood. A handful of mud. There, my dear. She was skinny but she was pretty. Gone.
CIG	He always tells that story.
NAILS	How long's he not staying for?
WRECK	Did you know my son was killed? I won't take it. He gave his life bringing the truth. They've got graves to go to. You have. And whose fault is it? I'm not saying.
DRUNK	Want a drink?
WRECK	I can't stop crying. Oh god. Yes please. I'm sorry, I'm sorry. Sending another one off to be killed? If you love me. If you get the chance. With me. Zig zig zig.

The WOMAN WITH A LIMP *comes back.*

LIMP   (*To* DRUNK.) Asleep.

WRECK   Just a bit overweight. Jellybelly,
                doubletrouble. Another thing, I've
                been hurt. A lot. Bastards. (*Pulling up
                his shirt.*) I got I got… Help me. Like
                a bite. Pus. With disinfectant. Could
                make me end up dead.

DRUNK   There then.

CIG   I don't need this.

LIMP   I could be really happy to be dead.
                Have some peace. She'll forget all
                about me. It's lovely there. Music
                day and night. Forever.

SPEEDY   I expect to be nothing. I pushed her
                in and… and someone… I didn't
                raise my voice. They want to destroy
                us, remember that.

LIMP   How long's forever?

DRUNK   What?

WRECK   I want to see him. Where's everyone
                gone? The people I love. Where is
                he? Go and get him.

                Doorbell. The SPEEDY YOUNG
                MAN *has the gun again. The* YOUNG
                WOMAN WITH A CIGARETTE
                takes it from him.

SPEEDY   Yes. Do it.

CIG	I don't want to do it.
SPEEDY	You can.
CIG	Yes. Good. I don't want to. Yes.
NAILS	And?
DRUNK	Zig zig zig.
NAILS	Come in.

The MAN WHO BITES HIS NAILS *starts to open the front door.*

Black.

End.

A Nick Hern Book

Ding Dong the Wicked first published as a paperback original in 2012
by Nick Hern Books Limited, The Glasshouse, 49a Goldhawk Road,
London W12 8QP, in association with the Royal Court Theatre,
London

Ding Dong the Wicked copyright © 2012 Caryl Churchill Limited

Caryl Churchill has asserted her right to be identified as the author of
this work

Cover image: John Stortz
Cover design: Ned Hoste, 2H

Typeset by Nick Hern Books, London
Printed in Great Britain by Mimeo Ltd, Huntingdon, Cambridgeshire
PE29 6XX

A CIP catalogue record for this book is available from the
British Library

ISBN   978 1 84842 303 9